JOSEF HAYDN

his greatest

PIANO SOLOS

A Comprehensive Collection Of His World Famous Works

IN THEIR ORIGINAL FORM

ARIETTAS

MINUETS

PIANO WORKS

VARIATIONS

SONATAS

SYMPHONIC EXCERPTS

Compiled by

ALEXANDER SHEALY

JOSEF HAYDN

Born Rohrau, Austria, March 31, 1732
Died Vienna, Austria, May 31, 1809

HAYDN (pronounced Hy-dn) is popularly known as "the father of the symphony and instrumental quartet".

Haydn's father (a wheelwright) and mother (a cook for the Lord of Rohrau) were both good singers who supplemented their small earnings by singing for festal occasions. When Franz was only five, he joined them in some of their concerts, playing a home-made sort of fiddle. By consent of Haydn's parents, he became a ward of his cousin, Franck, in Hamburg. There he was taught violin and other instruments, also Latin (for understanding sacred text).

In 1750, at age 18, Haydn composed his first instrumental quartet, which was received in great favor. Some eight years later, he was appointed musical director of the Chapel of Prince Esterhazy, where he subsequently composed many marvelous symphonies, masterly quartets and many highly esteemed instrumental pieces, sonatas and light concert works.

Having been acclaimed for many years in Austria, Germany, Italy, and indeed all through Europe, he accepted a concert offer in England in 1791 receiving a most cordial reception. His fame spread throughout the world.

Among Haydn's master-works are an oratorio "The Creation" and a cantata "The Seasons", which will be sung as long as there are people who love great music.

ALEXANDER SHEALY

CONTENTS

GYPSY RONDO

JOSEF HAYDN

Presto

sempre scherzando

6

staccato sempre

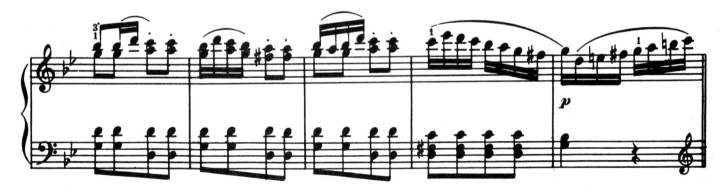

8

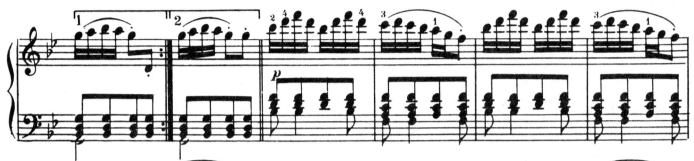

OXEN MINUET

JOSEF HAYDN

Moderato

Trio

D.C. al Fine

ALBUM LEAF

JOSEF HAYDN

Allegretto

SONATA IN G

(No. 1)

Allegro con brio

JOSEF HAYDN

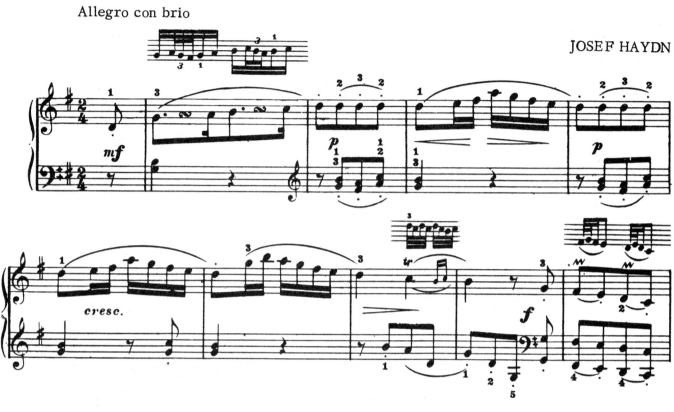

a) In the original this group of 32 ds. is always indicated by a turn, thus   *b*)

16

a) Although in the original, mordents are written, they must, of course, be short trills.

b) Make a slight pause after the hold.

Menuetto

a) These turns are always played with the last note of the accompanying group; therefore in this measure the turn is to be played with the third note of the second quarter.

b) Proceed without further waiting.

Trio.

a)   b)   c) Same as at (b   *Menuetto D.C.*

Presto

(Var. I)

(Var.II)

(Var.III)

(Var. IV)

MEDITATION

JOSEF HAYDN

Andante grazioso

ALLEGRETTO

JOSEF HAYDN

Allegro

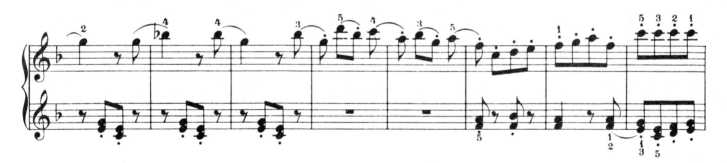

OXFORD SYMPHONY
(Excerpts)

JOSEF HAYDN

Presto ma non troppo

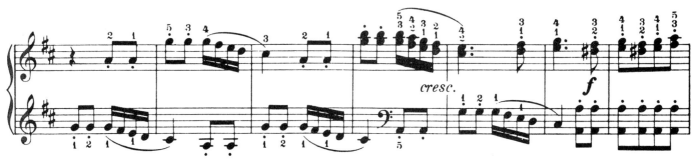

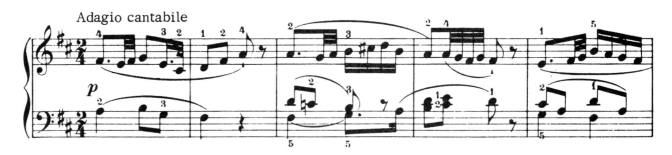

Adagio cantabile

Vivace

Allegro

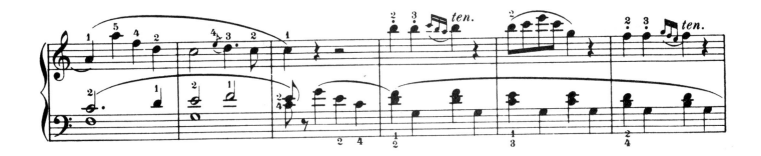

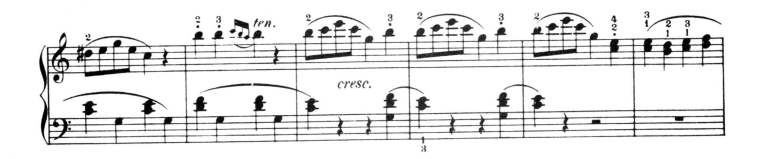

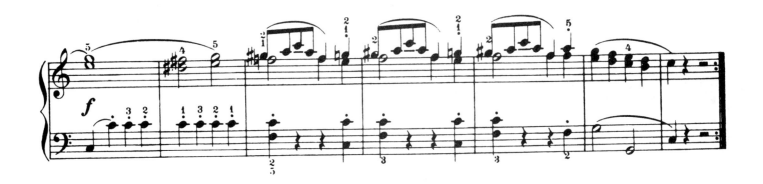

JOSEF HAYDN

Andantino un poco allegretto

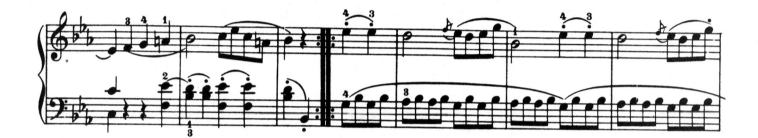

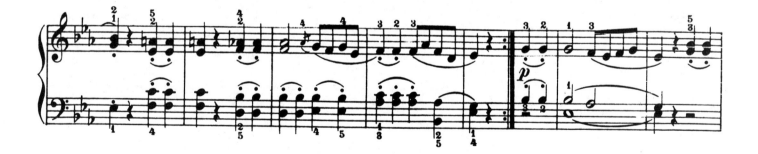

JOSEF HAYDN

Allegretto

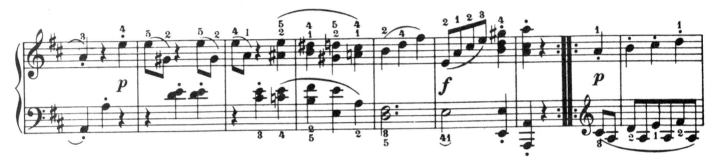

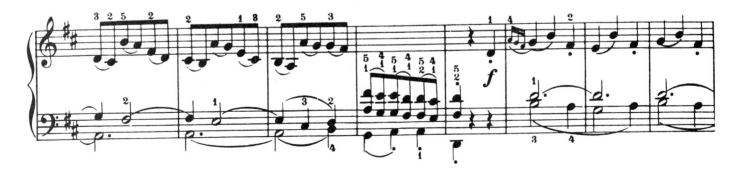

31

Fine

Trio

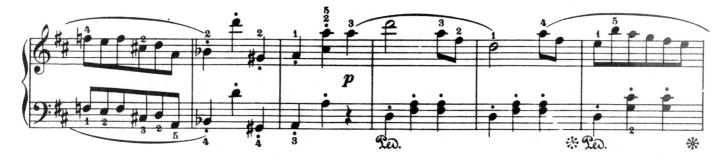

Menuetto D. C.

JOSEF HAYDN

Allegretto

Fine

Trio

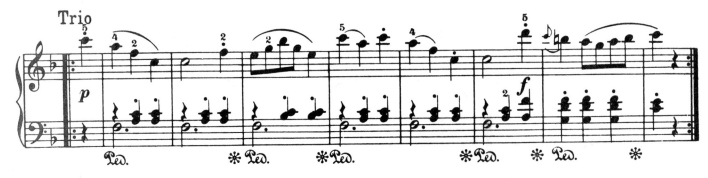

Menuetto D. C.

JOSEF HAYDN

Vivace assai

Fine

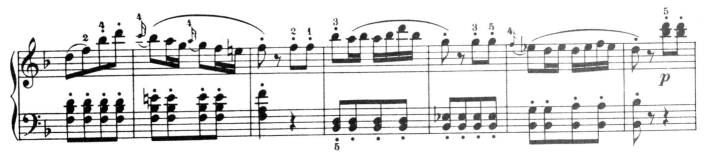

Da Capo, ma senza replica

JOSEF HAYDN

Andante con moto

SURPRISE SYMPHONY THEME
(Also in "Oxford Symphony")

JOSEF HAYDN

Moderato con moto

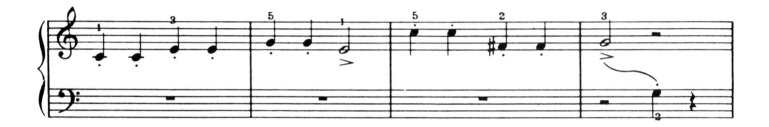

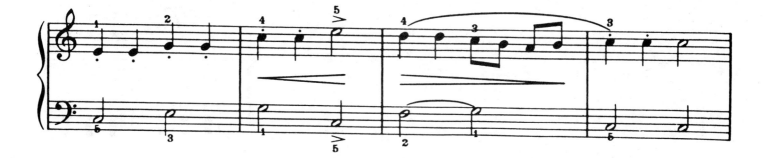

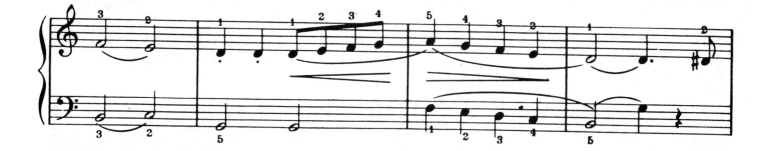

ARIETTA IN E FLAT

JOSEF HAYDN

Moderato

p dolce

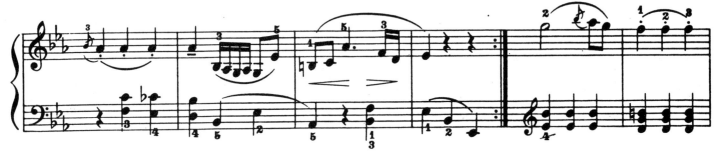

39

VARIATION I

VARIATION II

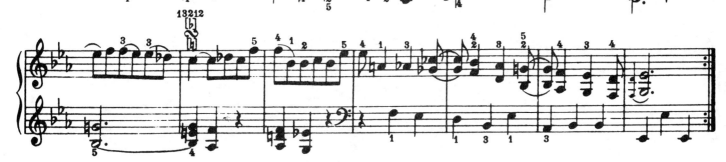

VARIATION III

VARIATION IV

VARIATION V

VARIATION VI

VARIATION VII

VARIATION VIII

VARIATION IX

VARIATION X

VARIATION XI

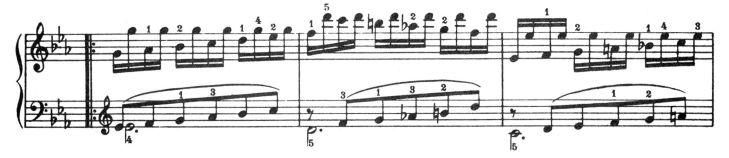

ARIETTA

THEME
Allegretto

JOSEF HAYDN

VARIATION I

VARIATION II

VARIATION III

VARIATION IV

VARIATION V

VARIATION VI

VARIATION VII

VARIATION VIII

VARIATION IX

VARIATION X

VARIATION XI

VARIATION XII

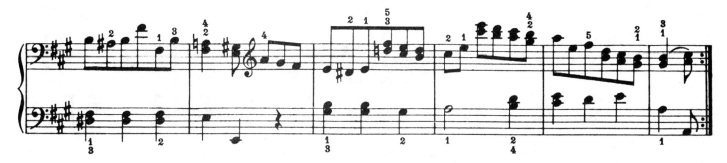

VARIATION XIII

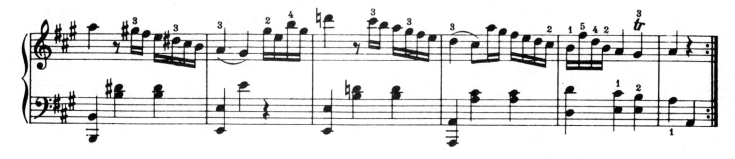

54

VARIATION XIV

VARIATION XV

VARIATION XVI

VARIATION XVII

VARIATION XVIII

MINUET IN A

JOSEF HAYDN

Moderato

f con energia

(imitando un corno)

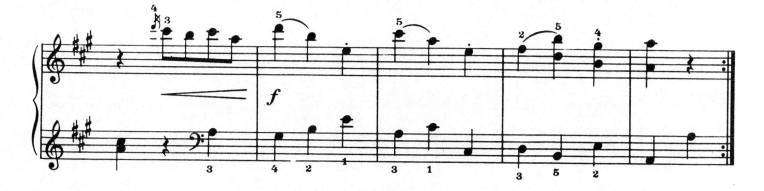

f

MINUET IN E
(No. 1)

JOSEF HAYDN

Trio
Minore

LA ROXELANE
(Air with Variations)

THEME
Allegretto

JOSEF HAYDN

VARIATION I

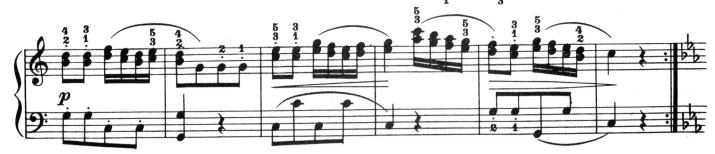

VARIATION II

VARIATION III

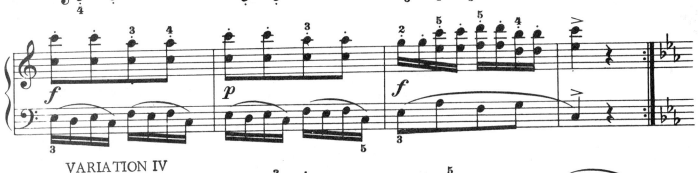

VARIATION IV

VARIATION V

MINUET IN E
(No. 2)

JOSEF HAYDN

Allegro e risoluto

(imitando)

MINUET IN B FLAT

JOSEF HAYDN

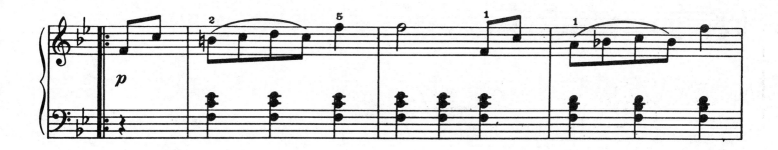

MINUET IN E FLAT

JOSEF HAYDN

Allegro e risoluto

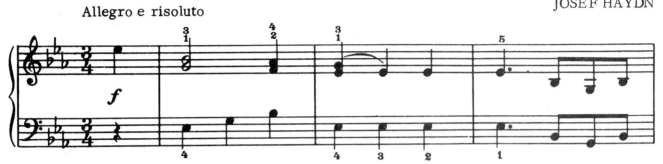

TRIO

p dolce e con delicatezza

MINUET IN C
(No. 1)

JOSEF HAYDN

Allegro giocoso

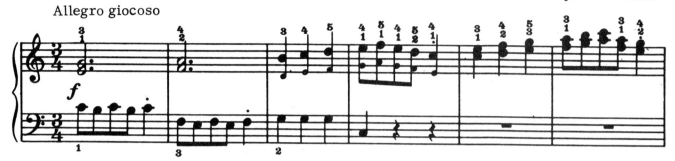

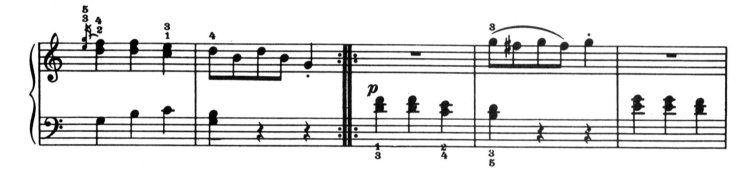

TRIO

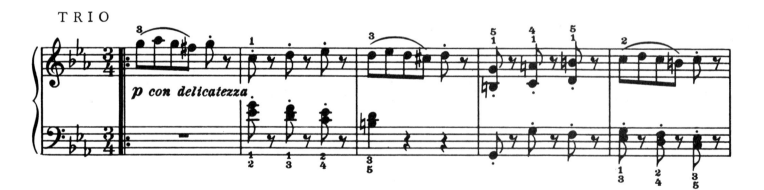

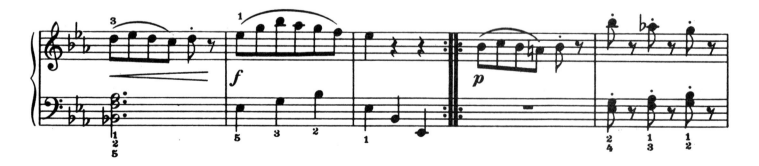

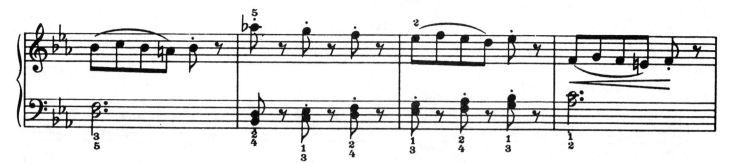

MINUET IN D
No. 1

JOSEF HAYDN

Allegro con brio

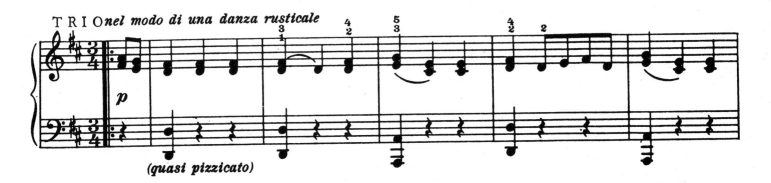

TRIO *nel modo di una danza rusticale*

(quasi pizzicato)

(quasi arco)

(quasi pizzicato)

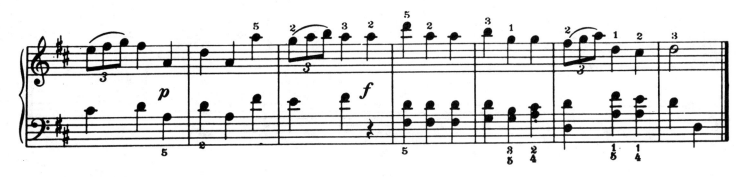

MINUET IN D

No. 2

Allegro vivace

JOSEF HAYDN

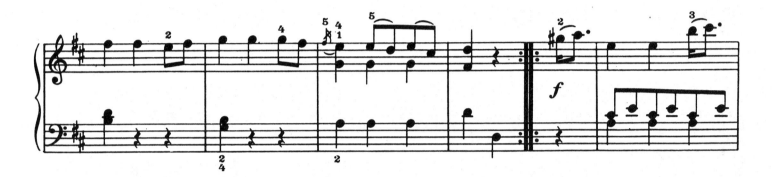

TRIO

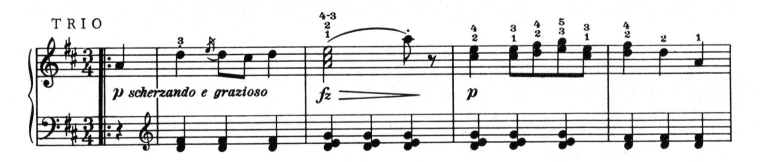

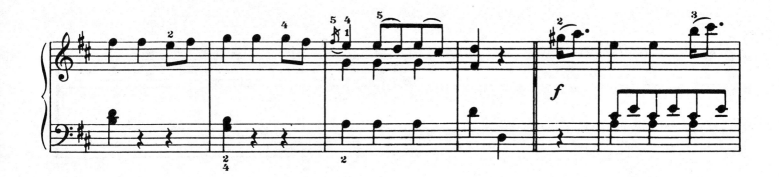

MINUET IN D
No. 3

JOSEF HAYDN

Allegro maestoso

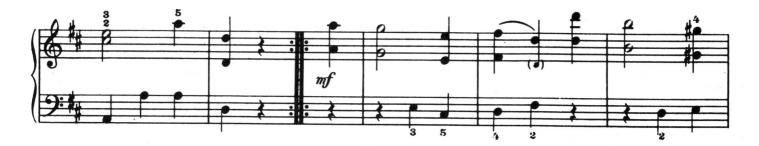

TRIO *scherzando*

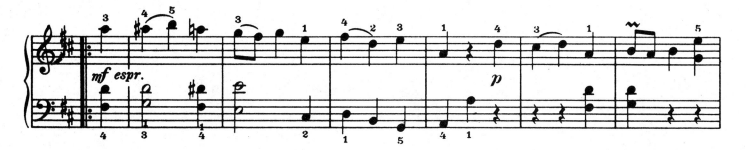

MINUET IN C
(No. 2)

JOSEF HAYDN

Allegro

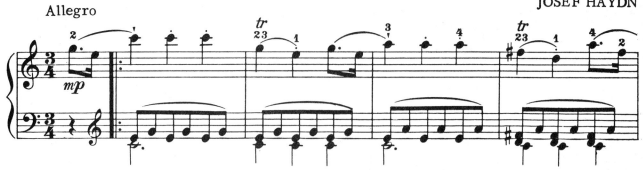

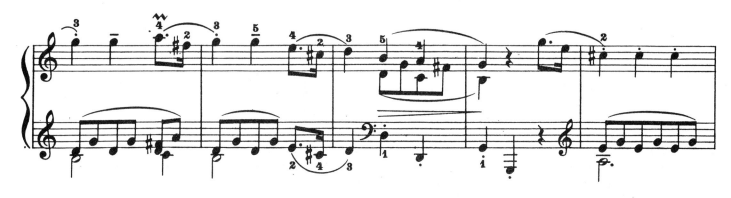

MINUET IN F

JOSEF HAYDN

ANDANTE
(with Variations)

JOSEF HAYDN

Andante

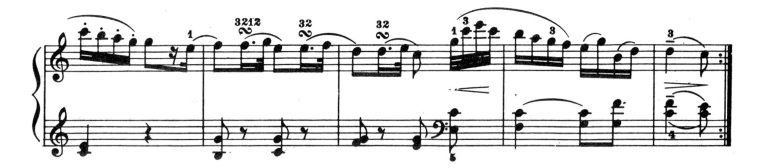

VARIATION I

VARIATION II

VARIATION III

VARIATION IV

VARIATION V
Minore

VARIATION VI
Maggiore

CAPRICCIO

JOSEF HAYDN

Moderato

94

FANTASIA

JOSEF HAYDN

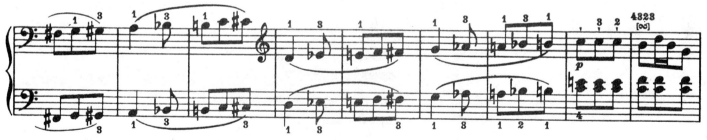

tenuto intanto, finche non si sente più il suono.

DANCE CAPRICE

JOSEF HAYDN

Andante

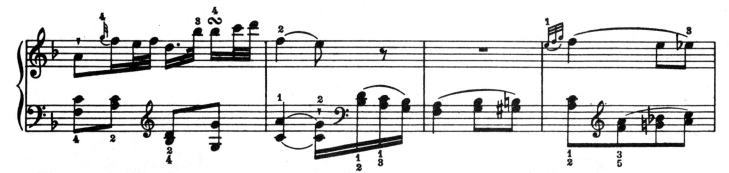

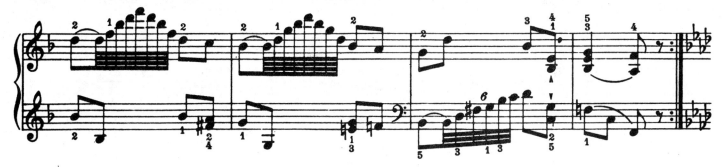

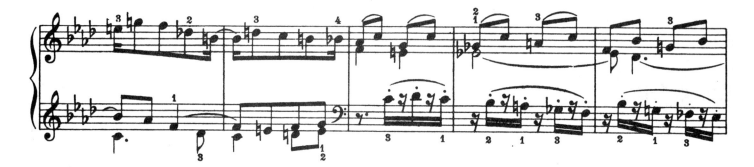

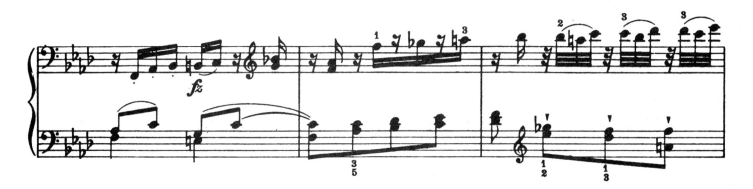

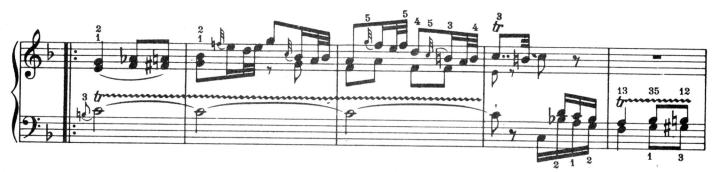

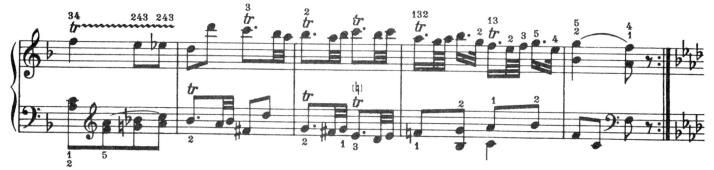

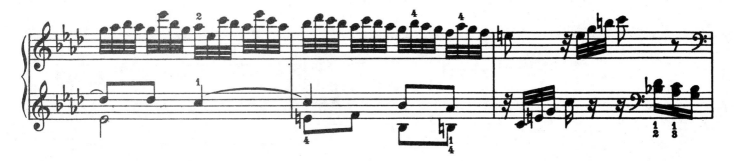

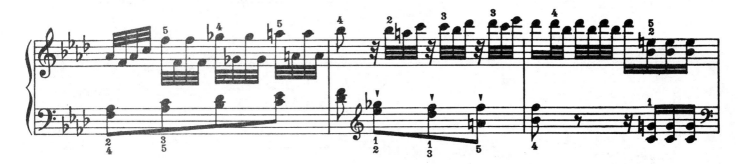

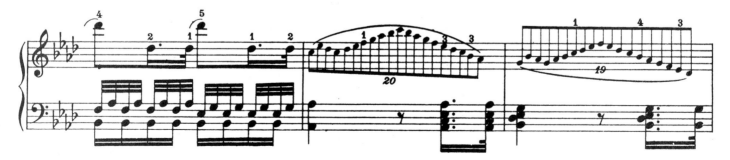

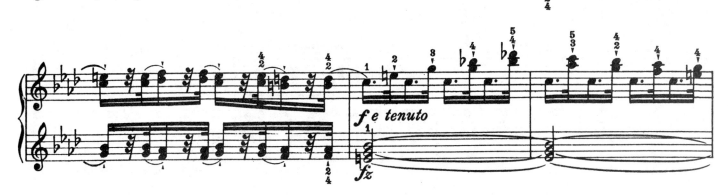

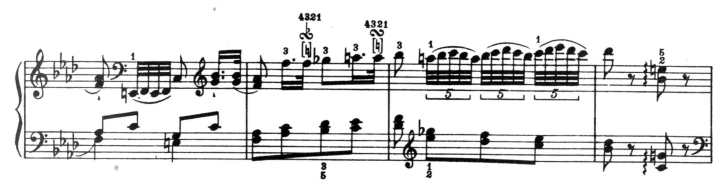

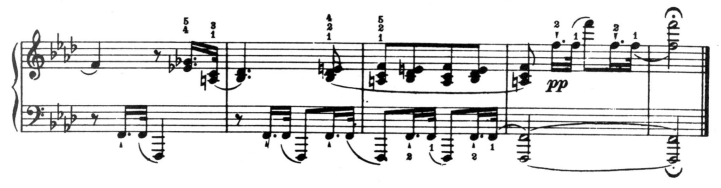

ANDANTE
(From "Sonata in C")

JOSEF HAYDN

Andante

SONATA E MINOR

JOSEF HAYDN

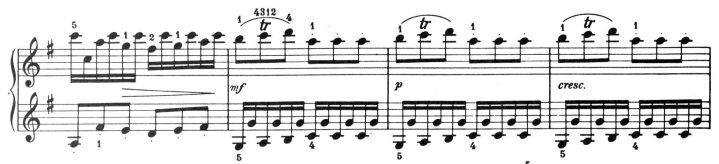

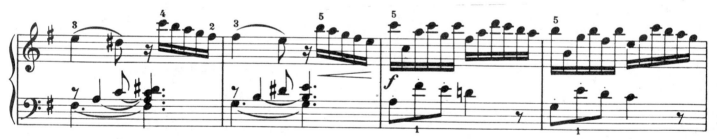

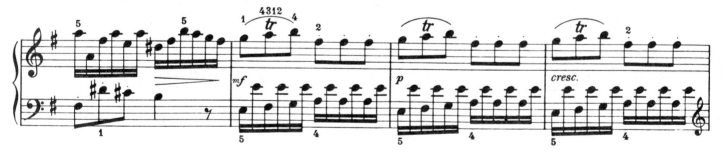

Adagio

mezza voce

mf   *perdendosi*

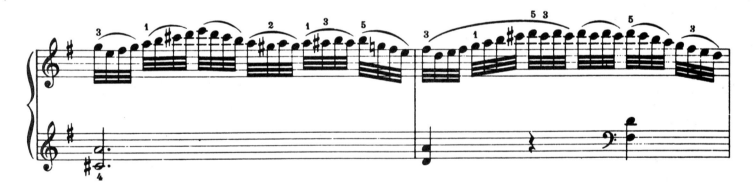

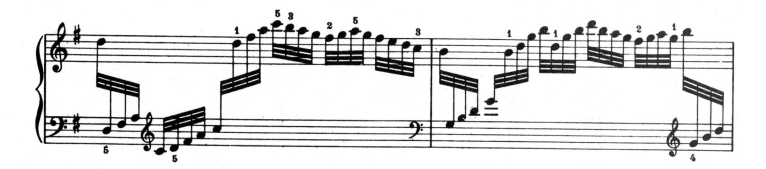

più Adagio

attacca subito

FINALE
Molto vivace

128

SONATA IN E FLAT

JOSEF HAYDN

Allegro moderato

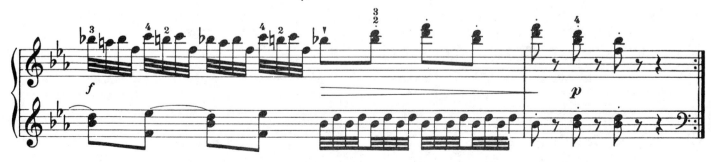

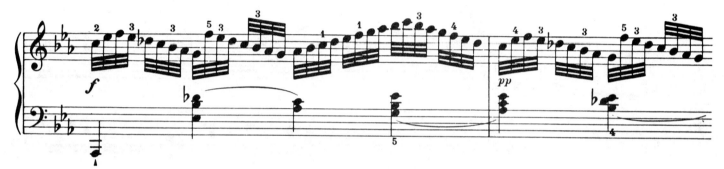

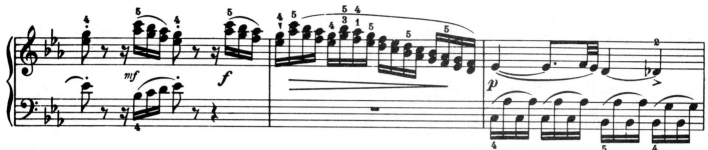

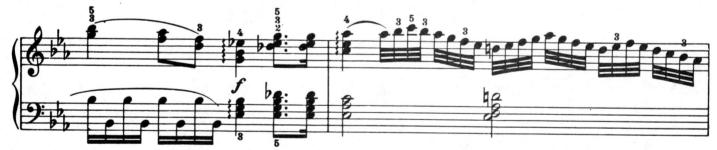

Adagio

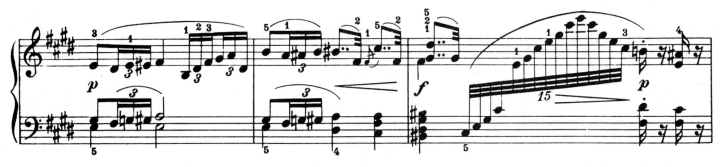

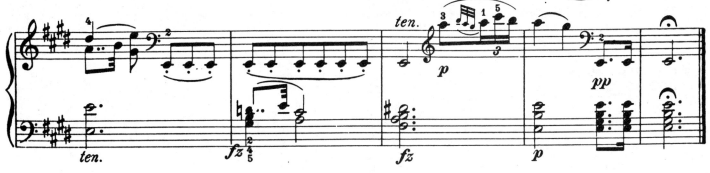

FINALE
Presto

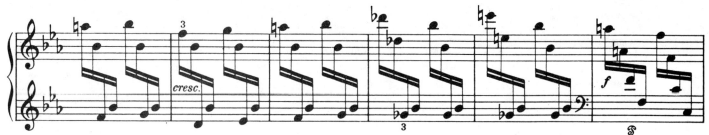

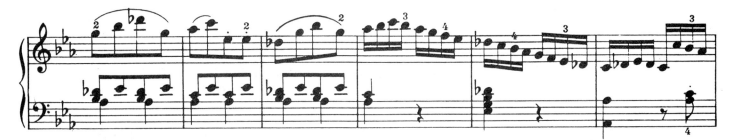

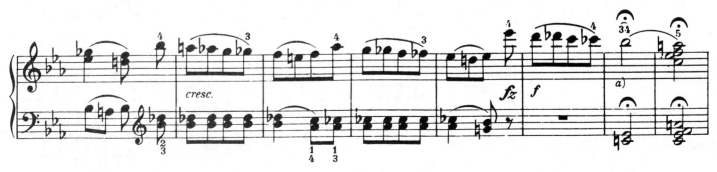

Adagio

Tempo I

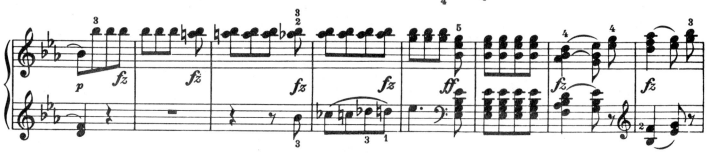

SONATA IN D

Allegro con brio

JOSEF HAYDN

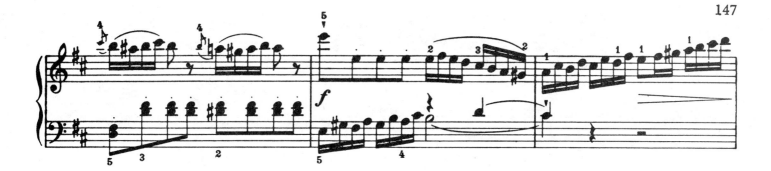

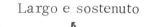
Largo e sostenuto

Attacca subito il Finale

FINALE
Presto ma non troppo

pinnocentemente

SONATA G MINOR

JOSEF HAYDN

Moderato

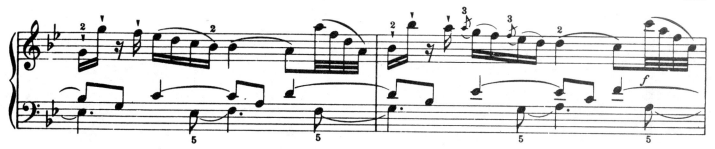

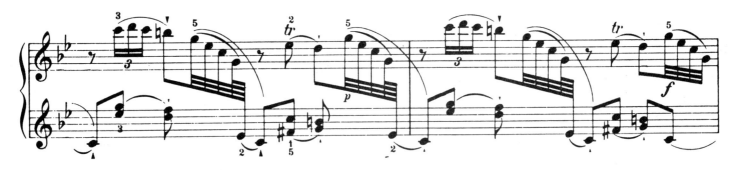

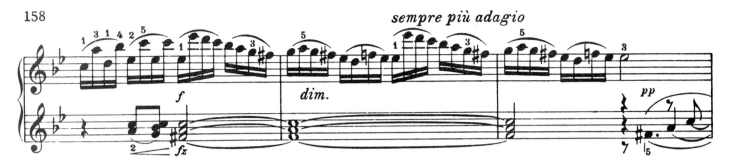

160

SONATA IN A FLAT

JOSEF HAYDN

Allegro moderato

Adagio

169

FINALE
Presto

SONATA IN C SHARP MINOR

JOSEF HAYDN

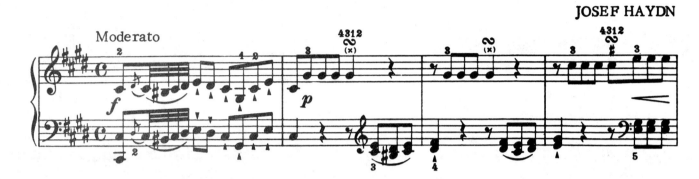

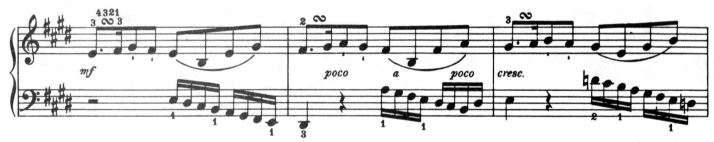

Scherzando
(Allegro con brio)

179

Menuetto moderato

TRIO

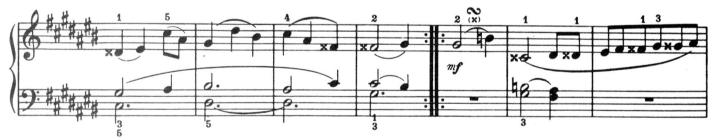

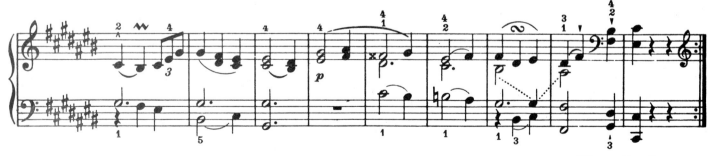

Menuetto da capo

A LITTLE WALTZ

JOSEF HAYDN

Con anima

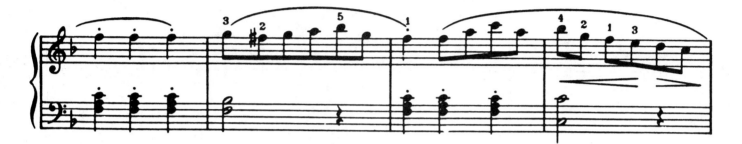

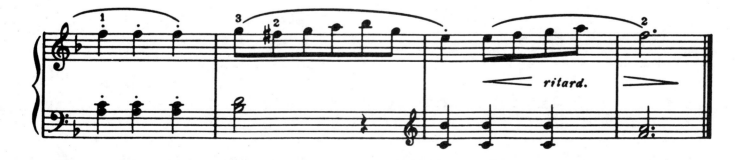

COUNTRY DANCE

JOSEF HAYDN

SONATA IN G

No. 2

JOSEF HAYDN

Allegretto innocente

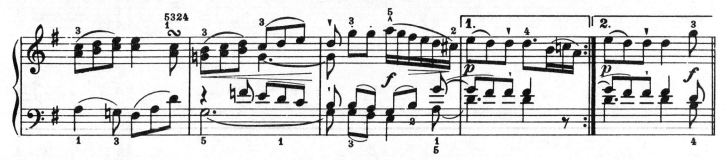

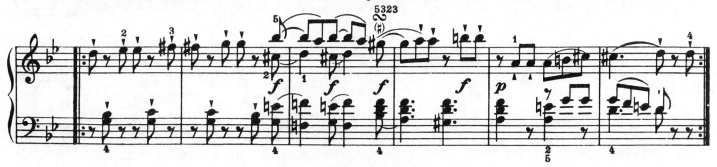